Devotions from the Nursery

Devotions from the Nursery

SASHA GARDINER

RESOURCE *Publications* • Eugene, Oregon

DEVOTIONS FROM THE NURSERY

Resource Publications
An Imprint of Wipf and Stock Publishers
199 W. 8th Ave., Suite 3
Eugene, OR 97401

www.wipfandstock.com

PAPERBACK ISBN: 978-1-6667-5493-3
HARDCOVER ISBN: 978-1-6667-5494-0
EBOOK ISBN: 978-1-6667-5495-7

VERSION NUMBER 102622

Contents

There Was an Old Woman Who Lived in a Shoe | 1

Little Miss Muffet | 2

Diddle Diddle Dumpling, My Son John | 3

There Was a Little Girl | 4

The Itsy Bitsy Spider | 5

Jack Sprat | 6

Baa Baa, Black Sheep | 7

Doctor Foster | 8

Tweedledum and Tweedledee | 9

Rain, Rain, Go Away | 10

Ding Dong Bell | 11

Do You Know the Muffin Man? | 12

Solomon Grundy | 13

Old King Cole | 14

Cobbler, Cobbler, Mend My Shoe | 15

Pease Porridge | 16

Hickory Dickory Dock | 17

Jack, Be Nimble | 18

Once I Caught a Fish Alive | 19

Little Boy Blue | 20

London Bridge Is Falling Down | 22

When I Was a Bachelor | 24

Elsie Marley | 26

Three Blind Mice | 27

Star Light, Star Bright | 28

Grand Old Duke of York | 29

Little Bo Peep | 31

Humpty Dumpty | 32

Pat-a-Cake | 33

Georgie Porgie | 34

There Was an Old Woman Who Lived in a Shoe

There was an old woman who lived in a shoe.
She had so many children, she didn't know what to do.
She gave them some broth without any bread;
She whipped them all soundly and sent them to bed.

The mother in this poem had so many children that she became overwhelmed. I can just imagine her being stressed and tired, and it seems she had no one to help her manage her many responsibilities. Unfortunately, it appears she might even have been in financial straits because she fed her children broth—which is basically liquid without meat or vegetables—without even any bread. It's apparent that her stress levels were also skyrocketing because she scolded her hungry children before putting them to bed. Only a mother in dire straits would scold a hungry child. Their hunger might have even escalated her feelings of frustration and inadequacy.

Does this situation feel familiar to you? Have you been struggling with your children or some other situation, and it feels like there is no help in sight? This is when we need to go to God. God will supply all our needs. We are reminded to bring all our troubles to God. When we turn to God, we can rest assured that God cares and will provide.

Be careful for nothing; but in every thing by prayer and supplication with thanksgiving let your requests be made known unto God.
—Philippians 4:6

Consider the ravens: for they neither sow nor reap; which neither have storehouse nor barn; and God feedeth them: how much more are ye better than the fowls? —Luke 12:24

1

Little Miss Muffet

Little Miss Muffet sat on a tuffet,
Eating her curds and whey;
Along came a spider, who sat down beside her,
And frightened Miss Muffet away.

Miss Muffet was minding her own business when she was approached and frightened so badly that she left her seat and ran away, leaving her food behind. Miss Muffet's food represents us focusing on Jesus by reading the Bible and meditating on Scripture. Her tuffet represents the foundation we have in God. The spider coming along represents the people or events in life that can provoke us to abandon God.

Many times, in life we are walking with God and focused on becoming better versions of ourselves. Then out of nowhere we are struck down by financial difficulties. Or maybe a relationship is broken, and our health begins to dangerously decline.

We are so frightened and full of anxiety we run away from God instead of drawing closer. We forget that before these difficulties arrived, we were taking sustenance for our body through the Bible and scriptures.

When you are frightened to leave God, pause, and allow the Holy Spirit to guide you. Do not let situations distract you from taking care of yourself so that you can be your best self.

There hath no temptation taken you but such as is common to man:
but God is faithful, who will not suffer you to be tempted above that
ye are able; but will with the temptation also make a way to escape,
that ye may be able to bear it. —1 Corinthians 10:13

Put on the whole armour of God, that ye may be able
to stand against the wiles of the devil. —Ephesians 6:11

Diddle Diddle Dumpling, My Son John

Diddle, diddle, dumpling, my son John,
Went to bed with his trousers on;
One shoe off, and the other shoe on,
Diddle, diddle, dumpling, my son John.

John obviously had a long day if he went to bed wearing his clothes. Though we don't know the age, he could have been a young child tired from playing hard all day and perhaps even from being corrected repeatedly.

"No, don't touch that."
"No, sit down."
"No, don't pull the cat's tail."

If John is tired, just imagine his poor parents or teachers. When our children are their most challenging, we must remember that they are a blessing. As they explore their world, we must gather patience and set up boundaries to help them become competent, compassionate adults. Not every day will be perfect. Parents will often question their child-rearing skills. But in the end, every investment of time and effort will be worth it.

Train up a child in the way he should go: and when he is old,
he will not depart from it. —Proverbs 22:6

Rejoicing in hope; patient in tribulation; continuing instant in
prayer. —Romans 12:12

There Was a Little Girl

There was a little girl, who had a little curl,
Right in the middle of her forehead.
When she was good, she was very good indeed,
But when she was bad, she was horrid.

Some days we are impressed with our children's behavior. We pat ourselves on the back, thinking we are doing a good job. Then come the days when they are defiant and push our buttons until we want to scream. We question our parenting abilities and even wonder whether our decision to have children was right or not. It is in these moments that we need to have patience. We have been charged with guiding these little future adults. They are still learning to manage big emotions—emotions that sometimes cause even adults to struggle. At such times, we must ask the Holy Spirit for patience to see us through these stages in our children's lives. They are only children once. Reflect today on one change you can make to improve your patience when challenged by these future adults.

And let us not be weary in well doing: for in due season
we shall reap, if we faint not. —Galatians 6:9

Put on therefore, as the elect of God, holy and beloved,
bowels of mercies,
kindness, humbleness of mind, meekness, longsuffering.
—Colossians 3:12

Be ye strong therefore, and let not your hands be weak:
for your work shall be rewarded. —2 Chronicles 15:7

The Itsy Bitsy Spider

The itsy bitsy spider climbed up the water spout;
Down came the rain and washed the spider out;
Out came the sun and dried up all the rain;
And the itsy bitsy spider climbed up the spout again.

The spider had a goal of getting to the top of that waterspout, even after being washed down by the rain. So, she waited for the weather to clear before starting her journey again. She didn't give up. She wasn't deterred by a setback.

Sometimes we have goals that rainclouds destroy. This is the time we should put our faith in God while waiting for the rain to go away. This is the perfect time to regroup, pray, and adjust our steps as needed without changing our goals. We must continue towards our goals once the sun dries up the rain. We must persevere despite the struggles that come our way.

There are many devices in a man's heart; nevertheless the counsel of the Lord, that shall stand. —Proverbs 19:21

I can do all things through Christ which strengtheneth me.
—Philippians 4:13

Jack Sprat

Jack Sprat could eat no fat.
His wife could eat no lean.
And so betwixt them both, you see,
They licked the platter clean.

Let's peek into the household of Jack Sprat and his wife. Jack did not eat fatty foods, and his wife did not eat healthy. How then did the two of them share such an existence? Did Jack pray daily for his wife to eat better? Or did he pray for understanding? Maybe his wife prayed for Jack to stop nagging her about her food choices.

In our close relationships, something will always rub us the wrong way about the other person. At this point, we need to extend God's grace. Many times, God disapproves of what we are doing. Despite this, He extends His grace. Remember to extend grace today when frustration knocks at your door.

But unto every one of us is given grace according to the
measure of the gift of Christ. —Ephesians 4:7

For by grace are ye saved through faith; and that not of yourselves:
it is the gift of God:
Not of works, lest any man should boast. —Ephesians 2:8–9

Grace and peace be multiplied unto you through the knowledge of
God, and of Jesus our Lord. —2 Peter 1:2

Baa Baa, Black Sheep

Baa baa, black sheep, have you any wool?
Yes, sir; yes, sir; three bags full.
One for the master, and one for the dame,
And one for the little boy who lives down the lane.

The sheep has been grazing in the grass as its wool grows. Along comes a man requesting three bags of wool. The sheep is prepared and able to supply the wool.

The Bible teaches us to prepare ourselves for the second coming of Jesus Christ. We should do that just as naturally as the sheep grows wool. The growth of the wool is aided by the sheep eating and drinking. Similarly, we should nurture our souls by reading the Bible and applying Scripture to our lives. This helps us prepare for Jesus' coming even though we don't know exactly when He will return.

But of that day and hour knoweth no man, no, not the
angels of heaven, but my Father only.—Matthew 24:36

So Christ was once offered to bear the sins of many; and unto them
that look for him shall he appear the second time without sin unto
salvation. —Hebrews 9:28

And take heed to yourselves, lest at any time your hearts be
overcharged with surfeiting, and drunkenness, and cares of this life,
and so that day come upon you unawares. For as a snare shall it
come on all them that dwell on the face of the whole earth. Watch
ye therefore, and pray always, that ye may be accounted worthy to
escape all these things that shall come to pass, and to stand before
the Son of man. —Luke 21:34–36

Doctor Foster

Doctor Foster went to Gloucester in a shower of rain;
He stepped in a puddle right up to his middle,
And never went there again.

Many times, we ask God for signs, but we do not listen when those signs are given. Was Dr. Foster even supposed to be going to Gloucester? Why did he continue walking in a rainstorm? Why was his mind so far away that he did not see the puddle that was extremely deep? It took a dramatic event to stop him from going again. We do not want to be a Dr. Foster. Take the time today to truly seek direction from God and then to listen to what God has to say in response. Find a quiet moment to allow God to answer your questions and direct your steps each day.

My sheep hear my voice, and I know them, and they follow me: And I give unto them eternal life; and they shall never perish, neither shall any man pluck them out of my hand. —John 10:27–28

Shew me thy ways, O Lord; teach me thy paths. Lead me in thy truth, and teach me: for thou art the God of my salvation; on thee do I wait all the day. —Psalm 25:4–5

Tweedledum and Tweedledee

Tweedledum and Tweedledee agreed to have a battle;
For Tweedledum, said Tweedledee, had spoiled his nice new rattle.
Just then flew down a monstrous crow, as black as a tar-barrel;
Which frightened both the heroes so, they quite forgot their quarrel.

Do you find yourself making mountains out of molehills due to petty differences? Your anger rises quickly when it would be best to examine what really took place. When this happens, we miss the true enemy that is lurking until it is too late.

The twins were arguing over a rattle, something that was probably an easy fix, when they were startled by a large crow. The argument was quickly forgotten because it was time to band together to defeat the real enemy. Don't let small differences stop you from seeing your true friends who can help you defeat the looming enemy. Ask the Holy Spirit to give you discernment. Ask that your heart be opened so that you can receive wisdom and act appropriately.

If any of you lack wisdom, let him ask of God, that giveth to all men
liberally, and upbraideth not; and it shall be given him. —James 1:5

Give therefore thy servant an understanding heart to judge thy
people, that I may discern between good and bad: for who is able to
judge this thy so great a people? —I Kings 3:9

The heart of him that hath understanding seeketh knowledge:
But the mouth of fools feedeth on foolishness. —Proverbs 15:14

Rain, Rain, Go Away

Rain, rain, go away.
Come again some other day.
We want to go outside and play.
Come again some other day.

This classic rhyme has many variations, but all form the same message. The children are wishing the rain would stop so they can play outside.

Many times, we go through life quickly, rushing from place to place, event to event, and we consider anything that hampers our activity to be an annoyance. Do we ever stop to think that maybe those "annoyances" are an opportunity to pause and regroup? We often forget to take time to rest and reflect on our blessings from God. Yes, the rain may be preventing us from what we want to do now. But instead of being annoyed by the delay, take the opportunity to meditate on what makes life worth living.

He that handleth a matter wisely shall find good: and whoso
trusteth in the Lord, happy is he. —Proverbs 16:20

But now the Lord my God hath given me rest on every side, so that
there is neither adversary nor evil occurrent. —I Kings 5:4

Ding Dong Bell

Ding, dong, bell, pussy's in the well.
Who put her in? Little Johnny Flynn.
Who pulled her out? Little Tommy Stout.

Are there days when you feel you are doing your best, but you are still verbally attacked? Or maybe you are misunderstood, and others do not understand your purpose? They come and decide to throw you down a well—figuratively speaking—killing your spirit, energy, and drive. But little do they know that you are about to be rescued and returned to your rightful place. You will be restored with more than before. Know that Jesus will rescue you. He is the Saviour.

And I will bless them that bless thee, and curse him that curseth
thee: and in thee shall all families of the earth be blessed.
—Genesis 12:3

For he that biddeth him God speed is partaker of his evil deeds.
—2 John 1:11

Though I walk in the midst of trouble, thou wilt revive me: thou
shalt stretch forth thine hand against the wrath of mine enemies,
and thy right hand shall save me. —Psalm 138:7

Do You Know the Muffin Man?

Oh, do you know the muffin man, the muffin man, the muffin man,
Oh, do you know the muffin man that lives on Drury Lane?
Oh, yes, I know the muffin man, the muffin man, the muffin man,
Oh, yes, I know the muffin man that lives on Drury Lane.

A muffin is described as a baked bread that may or may not be sweet. It provides sustenance for the body. Jesus describes Himself as the Bread of Life.

This rhyme is reminiscent of asking whether we know Jesus. Sometimes, His teachings make us feel warm and satisfied inside. At other times, our souls are chastised as we come to know Him better. Knowing Jesus and accepting Him in our lives leads to our salvation. Ask yourself today, "Do I know Jesus?"

And Jesus said unto them, I am the bread of life: he that cometh to
me shall never hunger;
and he that believeth on me shall never thirst.
—John 6:35

Neither is there salvation in any other: for there is none other name
under heaven given among men, whereby we must be saved.
—Acts 4:12

Solomon Grundy

Solomon Grundy, born on a Monday,
Christened on Tuesday,
Married on Wednesday,
Took ill on Thursday,
Grew worse on Friday,
Died on Saturday,
Buried on Sunday.
That was the end of Solomon Grundy.

Life is precious, from the moment we are born to the moment we pass away. Other than getting married, we don't know what else Solomon Grundy might have done with his life. This is a reminder that we must make every day count.

We should do good. We should be fair and just. We should love our neighbors. We should take time for family and friends. At the end of our lives, we want to know for certain that we are headed to heaven; so we must accept Jesus as our Savior before it is too late. Take the time today to meditate on the good in your life. Perform a kind gesture. Practice self-care and tell family you love them. Life is precious. Life is short. Make the most of it.

For we are his workmanship, created in Christ Jesus unto good works, which God hath before ordained that we should walk in them. —Ephesians 2:10

And let ours also learn to maintain good works for necessary uses, that they be not unfruitful. —Titus 3:14

Old King Cole

Old King Cole was a merry old soul,
And a merry old soul was he;
He called for his pipe, and he called for his bowl,
And he called for his fiddlers three.
Every fiddler had a fiddle,
And a very fine fiddle had he;
Oh, there's none so rare, as can compare,
With King Cole and his fiddlers three.

King Cole was classified as "old" in the nursery rhyme. He was old and merry. We have to wonder if he was always happy or whether he learned to find happiness in life. It must have been stressful being a king and having so many duties, so many people depending on you. He may have been sad and depressed at times, weighed down by all his responsibilities. In those moments, perhaps he turned to God and placed his trust in the Most High. You, too, can learn to be a "merry" soul by casting your cares on God and asking for help. In this way, you learn to be happy as you get older, just like King Cole.

Cast thy burden upon the Lord, and he shall sustain thee:
he shall never
Suffer the righteous to be moved. —Psalm 55:22

Be glad in the Lord, and rejoice, ye righteous: and shout for joy,
all ye that are upright in heart. —Psalm 32:11

Cobbler, Cobbler, Mend My Shoe

Cobbler, cobbler, mend my shoe;
Get it done by half past two.
Half past two is much too late,
Get it done by half past eight,
Stitch it up and stitch it down,
And I'll give you half a crown.

We see a need for shoes to be repaired. First, the cobbler is told to have the shoes ready at 2:30, then 8:30, because 2:30 is too late. The owner of the shoe appears to be rushing the cobbler to do his job, even though the quality may diminish when the work is done in haste.

This is similar to how we rush God to see results. We might pray on Monday and tell God we want an answer by Thursday. We then pray again Monday evening and ask for our prayer to be answered on Wednesday. God no doubt raises an eyebrow and says, "Really now? Please remember good things come to those who wait; My time is not your time." In this instance we need to let the Master do the job in His time for a favorable outcome. After all, God is the expert.

The Lord is good unto them that wait for him,
to the soul that seeketh him.
It is good that a man should both hope and quietly
wait for the salvation of the Lord. —Lamentations 3:25–26

I waited patiently for the Lord; and he inclined unto me,
and heard my cry. —Psalm 40:1

Pease Porridge

Pease porridge hot, pease porridge cold,
Pease porridge in the pot, nine days old.
Some like it hot, some like it cold.
Some like it in the pot, nine days old.

What exactly is Pease Porridge? It is described as a pudding usually made from yellow split peas, water, salt, and cooked meat. When it is cold, it can be fried. This rhyme highlights the differences in people's preferences.

Do you ever look at someone and ask yourself why are they acting the way they are? You wonder why they can't just do everything your way. You become increasingly annoyed with their decisions until you are ready to blow up at them. In these instances, God asks us to avoid passing judgement and seek to understand the other individual. Maybe their way is right as well, even though it's not your preference.

A fool hath no delight in understanding, but that his heart may discover itself. —Proverbs 18:2

Judge not, that ye be not judged. For with what judgment ye judge, ye shall be judged: and with what measure ye mete, it shall be measured to you again. —Matthew 7:1–2

Follow peace with all men, and holiness, without which no man shall see the Lord. —Hebrews 12:14

Hickory Dickory Dock

Hickory dickory dock. The mouse went up the clock.
The clock struck one. The mouse went down.
Hickory dickory dock.
Tick tock, tick tock, tick tock, tick tock.

A mouse is climbing on a clock until it strikes one, then the mouse runs down again, obviously frightened by the sound of the clock. Are we like the mouse, frightened by time as it marches along? Perhaps we fear that we have not accomplished our goals of finishing school, being married, or having children. As time passes without seeing our desires accomplished, we tend to withdraw and become fearful, hiding from life. God has not given us a spirit of fear, so why retreat and dwell on your supposed lack of success? Keep on pressing forward because there is still time on the clock. Do not fear.

For God hath not given us the spirit of fear; but of power, and of love,
*and of a sound mind. —*2 Timothy 1:7

*Casting all your care upon him; for he careth for you. —*I Peter 5:7

Have not I commanded thee? Be strong and of a good courage; be
not afraid, neither be thou dismayed: for the Lord thy God is with
*thee whithersoever thou goest. —*Joshua 1:9

Jack, Be Nimble

Jack be nimble, Jack be quick,
Jack jump over the candlestick.

Have you ever faced a crisis in your life that appeared as dangerous as a raging forest fire? God stepped in and told you that it was only a candlestick, and He would help you navigate it safely. Obstacles that are placed in our lives can show how faithful God is, and that we only need to depend on God.

Is your forest fire really just a candlestick?

For I the Lord thy God will hold thy right hand, saying unto thee,
Fear not; I will help thee. —Isaiah 41:13

I will lift up mine eyes unto the hills, from whence cometh my help.
My help cometh from the Lord, which made heaven and earth.
—Psalm 121:1–2

Once I Caught a Fish Alive

One, two, three, four, five,
Once I caught a fish alive,
Six, Seven, Eight, Nine, Ten,
Then I threw him back again.
Why did you let him go?
Because he bit my finger so.
Which finger did he bite?
This little pinky on my right.

Someone took the time to catch a fish. How proud the fisherman probably was as he admired his catch. Then, suddenly, the fish bit him; so he let the fish go. What a disappointment!

Does this happen to those of us who are supposed to be fishers of men? Do we seek to bring others to Christ, then get bitten by their hostile attitude or hurtful words? When this happens, we are sometimes tempted to just let the person go—like the fisherman did in the nursery rhyme. However, instead of letting the fish go, we are to continue to fish until the fish returns to the net of God. Fishing need not be overt; it can be gentle and unassuming. Who are you about to let go because they bit you?

And Jesus said unto them, Come ye after me, and I will
make you to become fishers of men. —Mark 1:17

Go ye therefore, and teach all nations, baptizing them in the name
of the Father, and of the Son, and of the Holy Ghost. Teaching them
to observe all things whatsoever I have commanded you: and, lo, I
am with you always, even unto the end of the world. Amen.
—Matthew 28:19–20

Little Boy Blue

Little Boy Blue, come blow your horn,
The sheep's in the meadow, the cow's in the corn.
Where is that boy who looks after the sheep?
He's under a haystack, fast asleep.
Will you wake him? Oh no, not I,
For if I do, he'll surely cry.

Blue was asleep on the job, and his animals were going untended. The cows were trampling and eating the corn. When his whereabouts were questioned, his family knew he was sleeping, but they didn't want to disturb him because he would cry.

Have you ever woken up to go to work with an overwhelming feeling of weariness? Perhaps you laid there pressing your alarm multiple times as you tried to convince yourself you needed to go to work because you needed the money. You dressed and headed to work, but you weren't happy about it. You were depressed as you thought about the long hours that would pass before you returned home. These feelings represent a discontentment and perhaps even a hatred for your current position. You might even be depressed due to circumstances that you want to change but have no idea how to change them.

Little Boy Blue may have been experiencing this same multitude of emotions, which led him to fall asleep. What do we do when this is our daily life? We turn to God. We pray for direction to get out of our current situation and contentment until the situation improves. We ask God to show us the bright spot in each day so that we can get out of bed and be productive. Today, meditate on Jeremiah 29:11.

For I know the thoughts that I think toward you, saith the Lord,
thoughts of peace, and not of evil, to give you an expected end.
—Jeremiah 29:11

But as it is written, eye hath not seen, nor ear heard, neither have entered into the heart of man, the things which God hath prepared for them that love him. —1 Corinthians 2:9

London Bridge Is Falling Down

London Bridge is falling down, falling down, falling down,
London Bridge is falling down, my fair lady.
Build it up with wood and clay, wood and clay, wood and clay,
Build it up with wood and clay, my fair lady.
Wood and clay will wash away, wash away, wash away,
Wood and clay will wash away, my fair lady.
Build it up with bricks and mortar, bricks and mortar,
bricks and mortar,
Build it up with bricks and mortar, my fair lady.
Bricks and mortar will not stay, will not stay, will not stay,
Bricks and mortar will not stay, my fair lady.
Build it up with iron and steel, iron and steel, iron and steel,
Build it up with iron and steel, my fair lady.
Iron and steel will bend and bow, bend and bow, bend and bow,
Iron and steel will bend and bow, my fair lady.
Build it up with silver and gold, silver and gold, silver and gold,
Build it up with silver and gold, my fair lady.
Silver and gold will be stolen away, stolen away, stolen away,
Silver and gold will be stolen away, my fair lady.
Set a man to watch all night, watch all night, watch all night,
Set a man to watch all night, my fair lady.
Suppose the man should fall asleep, fall asleep, fall asleep,
Suppose the man should fall asleep? my fair lady.
Give him a pipe to smoke all night, smoke all night, smoke all night,
Give him a pipe to smoke all night, my fair lady.

This rhyme about London Bridge makes it most evident that we need God and should ask God to direct our path. First the bridge is built with wood and clay. Obviously, that's not the best combination because it will eventually wash away. Next the builders tried iron and steel. Sadly, they were informed that it would bend. Next, they considered silver and gold, which they were promptly told would be stolen. At their wits' end, they decided to just hire a guard.

How different it would have been if only they had consulted God in their decision making. Each building material was more costly than the next, and the final outcome would leave them bankrupt. We should reflect on how leaving God out of decisions costs us more with each option we employ without consulting the Most High. We are left spiritually bankrupt and become a shell, constantly seeking, and chasing expensive options when we only need to pause and consult God. As you go about your day, allow God to guide your decisions.

Trust in the Lord with all thine heart; and lean not unto thine own understanding. In all thy ways acknowledge him, and he shall direct thy paths. —Proverbs 3:5-6

Without counsel purposes are disappointed: but in the multitude of counsellors they are established. —Proverbs 15:22

A man's heart deviseth his way: but the Lord directeth his steps. —Proverbs 16:9

When I Was a Bachelor

When I was a bachelor I lived by myself;
And all the bread and cheese I got I laid up on the shelf.
The rats and the mice, they made such a strife,
I was forced to go to London to buy me a wife.
The streets were so bad and the lanes were so narrow,
I was forced to bring my wife home in a wheelbarrow.
The wheelbarrow broke and my wife had a fall;
Down came wheelbarrow, little wife and all.

The bachelor had difficulty living alone and feeding himself. It got so bad, that rodents took over his pantry. He then decided he needed a wife, so off he went to get one. He found a lovely lady in London and decided to marry her and bring her home via wheelbarrow. This wasn't the best mode of transportation as a wheel broke and his wife went tumbling into the street.

We can relate to several points in this rhyme, but one important lesson is that it is hard to do things by ourselves. The poor bachelor was allowing rodents to overrun his house. He realized he needed help, but he didn't properly prepare to receive that help because his helper (his new wife) ended up in the street.

Sometimes we seek help but do not lay the foundation. We pray to God, but when we receive what we ask for, we are not equipped to handle it and lose our blessing…it ends up falling in the street.

Think about what you are praying for today. Have you prepared for your blessing? How will you handle it once you receive it?

That ye be not slothful, but followers of them who through faith and patience inherit the promises. —Hebrews 6:12

Every prudent man dealeth with knowledge: but a fool layeth open his folly. — Proverbs 13:16

For which of you, intending to build a tower, sitteth not down first, and counteth the cost, whether he have sufficient to finish it? Lest haply, after he hath laid the foundation, and is not able to finish it, all that behold it begin to mock him, Saying, This man began to build, and was not able to finish. — Luke 14:28–30

Elsie Marley

Elsie Marley is grown so fine,
She won't get up to feed the swine,
But lies in bed till eight or nine.
Lazy Elsie Marley.

Elsie has advanced to a new station in life. Therefore, she doesn't feel that she must work as hard as she did before. In the poem, she is called lazy, but her actions also reflect ingratitude. God has blessed her with a life of luxury, but she has forgotten how she got there. The fact is that, even when we make it to the top, work is still required of us.

Have you reached a point in life for which you have been fervently praying? Do you look around and see answered prayers? If the answer is yes, what are you doing to show your gratefulness to God? Are you still thanking God? Are you still putting in the work of prayer, church, and Bible study? When we reach our point of blessing, we can become lazy in our walk with God. This is not the time to become lazy. This is the time to continue our walk and show continued gratitude.

O give thanks unto the Lord, for he is good: for his mercy endureth
for ever. —Psalm 107:1

Rejoice evermore. Pray without ceasing. In every thing give thanks:
for this is the will of God in Christ Jesus concerning you.
—1 Thessalonians 5:16–18

How long wilt thou sleep, O sluggard? when wilt thou arise out of
thy sleep? Yet a little sleep, a little slumber, a little folding of the
hands to sleep: So shall thy poverty come as one that travelleth, and
thy want as an armed man. —Proverbs 6:9–11

Three Blind Mice

Three blind mice. Three blind mice.
See how they run. See how they run.
They all ran after the farmer's wife,
Who cut off their tails with a carving knife.
Did you ever see such a sight in your life,
As three blind mice?

Have you ever been led astray by friends? Imagine how those mice felt when their tails were cut off. All three were blind, but they decided as a group that it would be a good idea to scare the farmer's wife. Did one mouse perhaps tell the others, "Hey, it's ok; we won't get caught. Our other senses will kick in." How wrong they were!

In Luke 6:39, Jesus asks, "Can one blind person lead another? Wont they both fall in a ditch?" The ditch for these mice was the loss of their tails. Have you been in a situation where you followed friends down a path of destruction? Whether it be lies, stealing or something else that pricked at your very soul and left you drowning in guilt, what were the consequences of these actions? Have you been able to ask God for forgiveness and reset your path to one of righteousness? If not, it's not too late. Ask God for forgiveness and start anew today. Even if you've lost your "tail," you can still be redeemed.

A prudent man concealeth knowledge: but the heart of
fools proclaimeth foolishness. —Proverbs 6:9–11

It is as sport to a fool to do mischief: but a man of
understanding hath wisdom. —Proverbs 10:23

Star Light, Star Bright

Star light, star bright,
First star I see tonight,
I wish I may, I wish I might
Have this wish I wish tonight.

Wish upon a star and have your dreams come true. How many of us looked to the stars as children and sent up our wishes? Our hearts and minds were focused on the wish becoming reality. The same intensity that we gave to those wishes should apply to our prayer life. Prayer is the time we spend with God giving Him thanks for our blessings and placing our requests in His lap. A prayer life eases our burdens and worries because, once we pray, we know God is listening and will act. Sometimes we forget to pray due to the demands of our day. It is easy to become distracted. The good news is that we can pray anywhere and anytime because this is our conversation with God. During our prayer time, we must also remember to listen to what God has to say in return. After all, conversations are between two people. Have you prayed today?

Hear me when I call, O God of my righteousness: thou hast enlarged me when I was in distress; have mercy upon me, and hear my prayer. —Psalm 4:1

The Lord is far from the wicked: but he heareth the prayer of the righteous. —Proverbs 15:29

Therefore I say unto you, What things soever ye desire, when ye pray, believe that ye receive them, and ye shall have them.
—Mark 11:24

Continue in prayer, and watch in the same with thanksgiving.
—Colossians 4:2

Grand Old Duke of York

Oh, the grand old Duke of York, he had ten thousand men.
He marched them up to the top of the hill, and he marched them
down again.
And when they were up, they were up; and when they were down,
they were down.
And when they were only half way up, they were neither up nor
down.

The Duke had his men marching up and down a hill continuously. Up they went. Down they went. Sometimes, they were neither up nor down. Do you find yourself following this pattern when it comes to following God's Word? Sometimes, you are able to apply biblical principles daily, and you are proud of yourself for your immersion in your faith for weeks on end. Then life starts to get busy. Slowly you neglect your prayer life. Bible reading falls to the wayside. Suddenly you wake up and realize you haven't read your Bible in weeks. You can't remember your last season of prayer and being with fellow believers is a thing of the past. You have fallen down the hill, but you shrug it off and remind yourself that life is busy and you'll get back up when you can. Or maybe you halfheartedly read a few Scriptures and say a quick prayer, because something is better than nothing.

When that happens, you are in between and comfortable in your spot. But is that really where you want to be? We are cautioned to not be lukewarm followers. We are urged to remain steadfast in our beliefs. Yes, life can be overwhelming and staying on top of our faith sometimes seems impossible. Today, I encourage you to stay on top by selecting one daily habit to strengthen your belief. After all, we don't want to be in between.

I know thy works, that thou art neither cold nor hot: I would thou
wert cold or hot.
So then because thou art lukewarm, and neither cold nor hot,

I will spue thee out of my mouth. —Revelations 3:15–16

Examine yourselves, whether ye be in the faith; prove your own selves. Know ye not your own selves, how that Jesus Christ is in you, except ye be reprobates? —2 Corinthians 13:5

Therefore to him that knoweth to do good, and doeth it not, to him it is sin. —James 4:17

Little Bo Peep

Little Bo-Peep has lost her sheep,
And doesn't know where to find them;
Leave them alone, And they'll come home,
wagging their tails behind them.

Imagine how frightened Little Bo Peep was to discover that all her sheep had gone missing. She was responsible for them, but she had neglected her duties. Was Bo Peep daydreaming or perhaps even napping? Regardless, the sheep were gone.

We can be like Little Bo Peep in many ways when we feel we've lost control of a situation. We panic. We become anxious. We become frightened. That is when we must put our trust in God. Bo Peep had to trust that her sheep would come back to her, and we must trust that God will help us right what has gone wrong. Your situation may seem bleak. Have faith that God will see you through.

And they that know thy name will put their trust in thee: for thou,
Lord, hast not forsaken them that seek thee. —Psalm 9:10

But we had the sentence of death in ourselves, that we should not
trust in ourselves, but in God which raiseth the dead. Who deliv-
ered us from so great a death, and doth deliver:
in whom we trust that he will yet deliver us.
—2 Corinthians 1:9–10

Thou wilt keep him in perfect peace, whose mind is stayed on thee:
because he trusteth in thee. Trust ye in the Lord for ever: for in the
Lord Jehovah is everlasting strength. —Isaiah 26:3–4

Humpty Dumpty

Humpty Dumpty sat on a wall.
Humpty Dumpty had a great fall.
All the king's horses and all the king's men
Couldn't put Humpty Dumpty together again.

Humpty Dumpty lay broken on the ground. Pain radiated through his body. Perhaps he was unconscious due to the agonizing pain that swept through him. The king came to help along with all his men. Sadly, they were not able to fix Humpty Dumpty. What an awful situation to be in.

Sometimes, we become broken in spirit; and we reach out to man to make us whole. When man is not able to fix us, we sink deeper into our brokenness. It is God who is the ultimate healer. Putting our trust in God will heal all our broken pieces. We only have to ask God for healing while meditating on the Word. These steps will heal what is broken within us and bring us to wholeness.

The Lord is nigh unto them that are of a broken heart; and saveth such as be of a contrite spirit. —Psalm 34:18

He healeth the broken in heart, and bindeth up their wounds. —Psalm 147:3

Come unto me, all ye that labour and are heavy laden, and I will give you rest. —Matthew 11:28

But they that wait upon the Lord shall renew their strength; they shall mount up with wings as eagles; they shall run, and not be weary; and they shall walk, and not faint. —Isaiah 40:31

Pat-a-Cake

Pat-a-cake, pat-a-cake, baker's man.
Bake me a cake as fast as you can.
Pat it and prick it and mark it with "B."
Put it in the oven for baby and me.

When a baby is screaming for us, how do we react? We quickly move towards the baby to discover what is wrong. In this rhyme, we can assume the baby is hungry and demanding to be fed since the baker is being asked to bake a cake for both the exhausted parent and the hungry baby as soon as possible. While a delicious cake will please the baby and give the parent an energy boost, they both must wait because baking a cake takes time.

This rhyme is a reminder of the times in life when we have problems screaming for our attention. We try our best to handle it quickly, but we just can't seem to resolve the problem on our own. We must then reach out to God, who is our "baker." God has a solution with our name on it, but He will show us that the process to fix the problem is just as important as the solution.

What problem is demanding your attention? What problem in your life needs a quick fix? Turn to God. Ask for assistance and trust the process because it will be resolved only with God's help.

And whatsoever ye shall ask in my name, that will I do, that the Father may be glorified in the Son. If ye shall ask any thing in my name, I will do it. —John 14:13–14

My help cometh from the Lord, which made heaven and earth.
—Psalm 121:2

Georgie Porgie

Georgie Porgie, pudding and pie,
Kissed the girls and made them cry.
When the boys came out to play,
Georgie Porgie ran away.

When Georgie looked across the playground and saw beautiful girls, he ran up to them and started to kiss them without permission. When the other boys came out, Georgie immediately ran away. Georgie knew his actions were wrong. Did he stop to think before he kissed those girls, or did he immediately act on his feelings?

The crying girls represent the hurt we cause others when we sin. Sin is rarely an act that affects only the sinner. It has ripple effects. We cause family and friends to become anxious, worried, and troubled when we live a life of sin. The boys coming out to play could reflect the Holy Spirit who convicts us to do better, who reminds us that we need to be wise and prudent in our actions. Before you make decisions today, ask the Holy Spirit to lead you in the right direction.

Now the works of the flesh are manifest, which are these; Adultery,
fornication, uncleanness, lasciviousness, Idolatry, witchcraft,
hatred, variance, emulations, wrath, strife, seditions, heresies,
Envyings, murders, drunkenness, revellings, and such like: of the
which I tell you before, as I have also told you in time past, that
they which do such things shall not inherit the kingdom of God.
—Galatians 5:19–21

But every man is tempted, when he is drawn away of his own lust,
and enticed.
Then when lust hath conceived, it bringeth forth sin: and sin,
when it is finished,
bringeth forth death. —James 1:14–15

*And the spirit of the Lord shall rest upon him, the spirit of wisdom
and understanding, the spirit of counsel and might, the spirit of
knowledge and of the fear of the Lord;
And shall make him of quick understanding in the fear of the Lord:
and he shall not judge after the sight of his eyes, neither reprove
after the hearing of his ears.* —Isaiah 11:2–3

www.ingramcontent.com/pod-product-compliance
Lightning Source LLC
Chambersburg PA
CBHW071752020426

42331CB00008B/2297